MW00748997

Kelsey,
Merry Christmas, 2014.
  Good luck in your vet work!
I may need you someday,

Bari
and his person,
Rita

Betsy Fainberg
&
Arf! Arf! Merlin!

Seven Nearly Perfect Pulik

Rita Sikes

Illustrated by Betsy Feinberg

Copyright © 2014 by Rita Sikes

All rights reserved.

No part of this book may be reproduced in any form or by any electronic or mechanical means including information storage and retrieval systems, without permission in writing from the publisher.

Printed in the United States of America

First Printing November 2014

ISBN 978-1-63443-160-6 Paperback

ISBN 978-1-63443-161-3 Hardcover

Published by: Book Services
4729 East Sunrise Drive #448
Tucson, AZ 85718
www.BookServices.us

Contents

Dedication

Dedicated to my best friend and husband, Jesse. Jesse suggested I could write and believed I could.

Thank you Gilbert Pearson for introducing me to the world of Pulik. To Barb Edwards for making Pulik a part of my life.

Then there are LuBove, Fred, Smokey, Billie, Suni, Missy and Bari, the best authors ever. They just needed me to do the typing.

Thank you to Merlin the chocolate Labrador wander-dog. Had I not wondered what Merlin was doing out wandering with Betsy, I would never have met Betsy and Michael Feinberg of Book Services. This inspiring couple has helped my dream grow into reality. Without them the impossible would not have been possible.

Happy herding to all,

Rita

Why Pulik

It was blind faith that my friend Gilbert Pearson knew what he was talking about that led five-year-old daughter, Kelly, and me to our first Puli, LuBove. Before LuBove came into our lives, I studied the history of the breed.

Pulik (the Hungarian plural of Puli) are considered to be a very old breed, with a history going back over 1,000 years, possibly much longer. They are one of three breeds of Hungarian sheepdogs. The Pulik is considered a "loose eyed" worker. These dogs are not as intense as the Border Collie when driving sheep. They have a reputation for being an intelligent, active, and agile breed that is somewhat suspicious of strangers. Somewhere I read that Pulik can be very independent and stubborn and will only accept strong-willed individuals as masters. What left field did that information come from? Whoever said that did not realize that Pulik do not have masters! Of course, I only learned that piece of information after 32 plus years of being owned by Pulik. So I will delve no further into their fascinating history. If you are interested, simply Google "Puli".

I have enjoyed watching my various Pulik create their stories over the years. They have each taught me lessons.

There are three things you must have if you share your life with a Puli:

A sense of humor.

A sense of humor.

A sense of humor.

Besides the above requirements, you need a very large dose of patience. Remember, with a Puli the coat does not make the dog. If cords don't fit into your lifestyle, then change it.

Why Pulik? As for the first three requirements, you must know that Pulik give you chuckles and grins when they prance through your life, surfing the countertop for leftovers, sprawling on the kitchen table so they can see out the window, or bouncing off the back of the sofa on the race from sofa, down the hall, to the bedroom. Then it is a bounce off the bed and a return trip. (The advantage of Pulik over cats is that Pulik don't tend to indulge in this kind of activity in the middle of the night.)

One male Puli, who shall remain anonymous, thought my leg was a tree and used it to mark his territory. Face it, I guess I was his territory. After all, Pulik do not belong to people. People belong to the Pulik.

My furry family of loyal and faithful Pulik has been worth every minute: The chuckles and grins, and then the heartache when, as they must, each one leaves for the Rainbow Bridge. As each one leaves, there is a little hole in place in my heart where no one else travels, but that is a part of the circle of life. I would not change a thing.

The Pack

4

The Pack
By Bari

Hi there! I'm Bari (Prestige's Sunshine Ziggy), supposedly the last of the nearly perfect Pulik that have pranced through the life of Mom, Pops, Sam and Kelly over the last 32 years. I am told I'm the last because Mom is 70 and Pops is 75. They claim they will be at least 80 and 85 by the time I get to the Rainbow Bridge and be too old for more of us. However, time will tell.

I have been appointed by those that came before me to introduce you to each of us.

Ch: Prydain LuBove C. D. (Luba Lu), the first of this pack, will entertain you with a story or two and then pass the pen on to the paws of some of the rest of us. Enjoy!

Prydain Surmo C. D. (Fred) was the one true friend of the pack. She had eyes only for Sam the boy kid. (Yep. Fred was a girl.)

Whidbey's Alorn C. D. (Smokey) arrived with Fred. Smokey made up for Fred's quiet ways by being the "Tigger" of the pack.

Wyldmore's Feature Storee (Billie) was the protector of the Sikes' flock. She would rather growl first and be friends later, but friends only on her terms.

Ch. Catsun Queen Suno Prydain (Suni) was the bedroom dog. He preferred lying between the pillows on the bed to anything else in the whole world. ("Suni" rhymes with "Sunny.")

Bubbleton's Millennium Celebration (Mille/ Missy) was the best people trainer of all.

I am last, but isn't there a saying about the best comes last? If there isn't, there should be.

Prestige's Sunshine Ziggy (Bari). Got my name Bari because I was to rescue the Mom person in this flock from some challenging times, just like Barry the St. Benard who rescued avalanche folks in the Alps. However, I'd like to think I got this name because I'm a Bari good dog.

Hope these missives bring a smile to your face, a chuckle to your lips, and leave pawprints on your heart.

Happy Herding,

Bari

Seven Nearly Perfect Pulik

The Noble Sheepherder

They're Not Sheep?

By Luba Lu

Hi there! My name is LuBove and I am a Puli. For those of you who wouldn't know a Puli from a Pooka, I am a Hungarian sheepdog, not an Irish hobgoblin. Since I am a sheepdog, it's a given that my job is to herd sheep. That's a no brainer. No matter what the breed of sheepdog, most of us take our job very seriously. So, true to my heritage, my life started on the natural trajectory of doing what I was bred to do.

When I was old enough to leave my Mom, I went to a wonderful home. It was a place where I got lots of belly rubs, and as I began to grow up my herding instinct kicked in.

My people were so accommodating that they even had three sheep in the house for me. These sheep were quite large for the house and all black. I chose the living room as my pen. My people didn't seem to give much direction, so when the time came, I figured (being an independent thinker), "All this herding must be left up to me."

I began by very close observation of my sheep. They had a tendency to give each other their own space. Somewhere I remembered dreaming about this task as told to me by my Grandfather. He was quite firm about the fact that sheep had to be gathered up and moved as a "flock." I guess that meant all bunched together and going in the same direction.

I really wanted to impress my people, so I started to practice this gathering operation when they were not home. I would bark and circle until all the sheep were in the center of the living room floor.

Practice, practice, practice. After about a week, the sheep got the idea, and all I had to do was start circling them and they would go bed down in the center of the floor.

They're Not Sheep?

Now on to step two. Granddad said they had to be driven somewhere. Now most of you realize a house isn't really large compared to a pasture, so my choices were limited.

While watching television one day with my people, I saw a dog put some sheep in a corner and then up a ramp into a semi-trailer truck. Well, no semi-truck here, but at least I could be ready for when that day arrived by getting my sheep into the corner.

When my people left the house, that was my big chance. I had to get one sheep off the bed and one away from the water trough; the last one was hiding under the kitchen table. Guess he knew that the great Luba Lu was about to strike. "Okay sheep! Head for the living room, and I mean it!"

This situation took a little more barking than usual, but before you knew it, the sheep were in the center of the living room floor. It took some snapping at hocks, but I finally got them bunched into the corner and lying down. I sat there in the center of the floor to be sure my sheep stayed put. But hard work calls for rest, and I accidently fell over and went to sleep. If the darned sheep had been more cooperative, I would not have been so tired.

11

My people came home and I promptly greeted them at the door and pranced into the living room to show them my great accomplishment. My lady got a funny look on her face and said to her husband, "Isn't that odd? The Newfies are all cuddled into the corner!" Then she walked off. No thank you or how-dee-do or "good dog" for all my work.

People are so fickle. I thought I had a great home. I certainly was doing my part to keep order. And what happened?! The next thing I know I was in the belly of an airplane headed for someplace called Wyoming.

As I was loaded up to go to the airport, my people said something about the Newfoundlands being intimidated by a Puli and that would not be good at a dog show. My people said they loved me and were sending me on to someone that needed me. I hope that someone has sheep.

"They're Not Sheep?"

"Maybe Wyoming has possibilities, after all."

The Middle of Nowhere
By Luba Lu

Hi there! Remember me? I'm the preeminent sheepherder who was excommunicated from sunny California, the renowned Luba Lu.

I couldn't believe it when my plane set down in Wyoming. Wind, wind, wind and miles of *nothing*. Do people even live here? Guess they must because when my crate was set down in the airport terminal, I was greeted by a kid peering into my crate door and squealing, "LuBa Lu, you are really mine!" Really hers? Doesn't this kid know Pulik don't belong to anyone?

Well! I was put into something they called a pick-up truck, and we headed east from Casper to Douglas, followed by 15 more miles south to a ranch. Wow! Got out at this ranch place and you couldn't even see any other houses.

I was about to tell this young girl kid who was boss, when out bounced a huge black sheep. The Mom figure called him Cujo and told him to be nice.

Oh goody! Another sheep to herd! Is it called herding if you only have one? It was black and lived in the house so it must be a sheep like those in the last place I lived, but it was awfully skinny. They must have just sheared this critter too. You couldn't make a gnat's sock out of the amount of wool on its body.

I might need to play this one a bit differently. After all, if I don't work out here, where would the next stop be? Siberia? Even more of nothing than this Wyoming place. I will leave Cujo alone for today.

Looking at my options, I decide the best bet is to suck up to the girl kid. A few licks and a flop on my back for a tummy scratch and she was *mine*. Tonight I get to sleep in her bed. It's a double bed. Know what? Bet I can make her sleep on the edge by morning?

Later. If you bet against me, you lost. Girl kid even had dog biscuits hidden in the bookcase headboard to sneak to me after the lights were out. This is turning out to have possibilities.

"I *do* look like a mop? Right?"

Cujo
By Luba Lu

The weeks have passed. My cords have grown out a bit, and I'll have to find a hairdresser in this barren Wyoming landscape pretty soon.

In the meantime, I have tried my best to herd the indoor sheep. After a great deal of observation, I have come to the conclusion that when you have a total of one sheep, it does not herd. I circled, I nipped hocks, I barked, I bit his nose, but Cujo just stood there ignoring all my efforts.

Finally one day the Boss Lady laughed and told me to give it up; Cujo was a Doberman Pinscher dog, not a sheep. I knew that. After all, Pulik know everything. (Well almost.)

After a night of restful sleep, I had a talk with Cujo. I told him I would leave him alone if only on occasion he would pretend to be a sheep. After all, I needed to stay in practice. Someday I might get a real chance to be a sheepdog.

It was shortly after this that I discovered that although he appeared to be really intelligent, Cujo did have a dumb side.

We were out checking the hay meadow. Wanted to be sure it was safe for horseback riding. On the way home Cujo wandered down by the creek. We got a cool drink and started to cross in a shallow spot.

That's when Cujo sounded the alarm. "Intruder, intruder!" he woofed. Well I didn't see one, but immediately went into my sheepdog guard mode. If I recall what Grandfather said, that meant "Get behind something and check the danger." So I got behind Cujo and pretended I was a kitchen mop. Certainly no one would expect a kitchen mop by a creek. Later I recalled that what Grandfather really said was, "Get up on a rock, something taller, and check out the danger." I think he also said something about making a plan, but at this moment there was no time for "a plan."

Cujo

With a giant leap Cujo was next to the intruder and began biting it. The intruder fought viciously. At least I thought it must have because Cujo began crying and running toward the house. I didn't have time to fight the intruder. After all it was my job to cover Cujo's back so to speak. I was right behind him.

Boss Lady heard the howls and headed for the yard. She was ready with gun in hand. Next thing I knew I was in the house and Cujo was in the pick-up. I heard the words "Vet, and this won't be fun." Darn, I get left out of everything.

Cujo came back walking like he had been drugged. I expected him to show up with a medal for being brave. I asked, "What on earth happened to you?" He slurred his answer. "Porcupines are squatters, not intruders. They get to stay." This was not good. My friend's mouth hurt. I licked his ears to help him feel better. Well, Cujo is a great friend, so I will always have his back because I am a brave, invincible Puli.

"Hands off da lady, ya bozo!"

Cujo's Road Trip
By Luba Lu

Four years have passed, and Cujo and I have come to a truce. About once a week I pretend he is a sheep, and he obediently goes to the corner of the living room. Then I make sure Boss Lady knows I have done my job.

Now we are friends, but a new wrinkle has come into the household arrangement. That wrinkle is a fella. For four years it has been Boss Lady, girl kid (Kelly), Cujo and me. Personally I thought we made a great team, but you know grown-up humans. They seem to think they need other grown-up humans.

I kept telling Cujo to be cool, but does he ever listen to me? Cujo tells me he was brought to the ranch to keep it safe, kinda like Hank the Cowdog. After all, this *is* out west and Boss Lady and Kelly were alone before he came along.

When anyone knocks at the door, Cujo goes ballistic. "Woof, growl, woof, growl." I tell him he should just let me do it; Pulik have a more important bark and the person will leave. But no, Cujo just carries on until Boss Lady says, "Nein." Then he quits. I sure don't get that.

Well, this fella and a boy kid persist in coming to the house. Every time they walk in the door, Cujo goes ballistic. Boy kid likes Cujo and Cujo likes boy kid, so all is well there.

However, fella is another story. Fella sits by Boss Lady on the sofa. That definitely does not sit well with Cujo. He plops down on his back side about 6 feet away and watches the fella, closely monitoring his behavior. If fella even moves, Cujo peels back his upper lip and lets out a low and ominous growl.

I try to herd Cujo away, but on this one, he simply will not back down. Boss Lady just laughs. Time flies, and I guess human people do something called getting married. Plans are made for this event, but fella is not happy. Boss Lady has to make a choice.

Suffice it to say, Cujo is now happy in Kentucky and fella is now Pops.

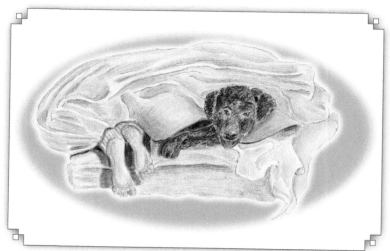

"I'll just sleep here at the foot of the bed."

The Kill Shot
By Fred

Hi there! Fred is my handle. Smokey and I were the second and third Pulik to arrive at the Sikes' house. Smokey was eighteen months old, and I was about three. When we first arrived at the ranch, Luba Lu met us and set us straight as to who was the boss. It made no difference to me, and Smokey was so immature he didn't even get the concept of leadership.

Luba Lu was definitely the girl kid's dog. Smokey attached himself to Pops and Mom and that left me. Later I found out that Smokey would attach himself to anyone who scratched his ears and told him he was good.

There I was, Fred the quiet nearly perfect Puli, without my own person. I really needed my own person. Boy kid didn't really seem interested, so I just plopped on Mom and Pops' bed and dreamed about having my own person. In my dreams, oddly enough, my own person looked exactly like the boy kid, whose name was Sam.

The second night in bed with Mom and Pops, I decided it was time to put my devious plan into action. I discussed this with Smokey and he agreed to help me. After all, Smokey wanted the whole bed. So on night two we both stretched, kicked and wiggled.

The next morning Mom came up with a theory. After the humans go to sleep, any dogs in bed grow to about four foot by four foot and push the humans to the edge of the bed. So now it was Pops' turn to come up with a plan.

On night three Pops went to Sam's bedroom and ask him to please keep me in there because I was taking up too much room. O-o-o-o-kay. Step one implemented and achieved.

Now on to step two: Sleep at the foot of the bed, out of the way. Sam gave me one pat and said,

The Kill Shot

"Goodnight Fred." I thought, "That's a start. He is at least speaking to me."

This was really difficult. I *so* wanted to get closer, but being the nearly perfect Puli I knew I had to bide my time.

The foot-of-the-bed deal lasted about three days. Next it was on to sleeping beside Sam. I got a few more pats here, so I knew I was making

"My very own person, at last!"

progress. Now it was time for the kill shot, the one that makes him know he belongs to me. He is mine and only mine.

One night, ever, ever so slowly I made it to the pillow. Voila! The kill shot. Sam is at the foot of the bed and I am Queen. This move got our conversation going.

I have since added another touch that makes me absolutely special as far as Sam is concerned. Each night at bedtime, before I go to the pillow, I go to the foot of the bed and clean his toes.

Life is good as the owner of a boy kid.

The Kill Shot

Tigger takes the form of a Puli.

Aussies
By Luba Lu

How quickly time passes! Fred has gone to the Rainbow Bridge, and Betty and Slim are to become part of the Sikes' family. So here I am, Luba Lu, the one-and-only First Puli, and I have two Australian Shepherd pups to train. Of course, I also have Smokey Puli, and I know he will be *such* a great help. I believe it is called, "Slim to none at all."

Betty is to be boy kid Sam's pup and Slim will belong to Pops. Naturally, since these whippersnappers are Aussies they will belong to the human people. That is not the case with we nearly perfect Pulik. No one owns us. Like cats, we correctly assume that people are here to serve us.

When Pops and Sam arrive with Slim and Betty, Mom oohs and ahs. These new kids are red colored with white paws and a white strip on their faces. They also have disappointingly short, practically nonexistent tails. However am I going to tug them where they are supposed to go? Oh well, I'll think about this; I'm sure I can come up with some method of teaching the Aussies the ropes.

Slim is quite independent, and when put down on the floor he starts sniffing and running around. Where are his manners? Doesn't he know that according to dog behavior 101, he should first get my approval. I am the matriarch, boss, head dog, honcho. What an upstart pup!

Betty hunkers down in the middle of the living room floor, eyes wide, ears tucked back. As I am observing this, in bounces Smokey.

Remember Tigger from *Winnie the Poo?* That's Smokey. Bouncy, trouncy, double flouncy. Smokey stops and lets out a Puli woof. (Puli woofs sound more important than other dog woofs.)

After one more jackrabbit hop, Smokey swings his head like a wrecking ball, and Betty is rolled over twice. I almost feel sorry for her. Betty emits a squeal. The Mom in this place takes charge and tells Smokey to settle down. Smokey, being an almost obedient Puli, runs for his dog crate. The crates are stacked two high, so Smokey has quite a leap to make it into the top crate.

Although observing all this made me more than a bit tired, it also got me to thinking. This situation has possibilities. Maybe goofy old Smokey could come in handy in the pup training, after all. Guess I'll hop on the sofa, take a nap and give this some thought. Nap? Who can nap? My mind begins to

"Gotcha!"

churn with ideas. All those ideas make me tireder than I thought. I can hardly keep my eyes open.

"Squeal, squeal!" What's all that yowling? I must have fallen asleep. What's all the kerfuffle?

I jerk awake just in time to see Smokey screech to a halt, then make an abrupt u-turn. Three giant strides, and I hear the crate bounce as Smokey hits the top rack. I look around for the Mom person. Did I miss her correction? Nope. Mom is nowhere in sight. As I lay myself down to ponder this unexpected development, I glance into the middle of the room, and I swear I see Betty grin. "Gotcha!"

Aussies

Billie's panic results in household chaos.

Where's Mom?
By Billie

One morning Mom gets up. She walks and feeds us as usual, but Pops doesn't go to work. How weird.

Next thing I know, Suni and I are in the dog crate. Long, dull hours pass, and here come the girls, Jessica and Rachael, along with their mom, Lesley, to take care of us. What on earth is going on? Where are Mom and Pops?

At the end of the day Pops returns, but no Mom. Days go by. Thursday. Friday. Saturday. Sunday. Still no Mom. "WHERE'S MOM? Hey, Pops, WHAT DID YOU DO WITH MOM?"

I know I'm not a large dog, but size shouldn't matter. He should listen to me. Something needs to be done. Pops is not paying attention. Well then! I'll get his attention!

It's Sunday morning and still no Mom. O.K. that's it! Time for action. I develop an emergency protocol designed to get Pops attention.

Pops is still in bed. I've waited long enough, maybe too long to save Mom. It's time to put my plan into action.

Step one: Creep stealthily off the bed.

Step two: Tear the toilet paper off the roll. A thousand pieces should be just about right.

Step three: Pops thinks that billfold is important. *I'll* show him important. This green stuff labeled $1.00, $10.00 and $20.00 tastes horrible, but a dog's got to do what a dog's got to do. A hundred pieces, more or less, of green confetti. Now *that* should get his attention.

I'd better have a snack on the leather piece all that stuff called money is stuffed into. The leather is like a cleansing mouthwash, compared to chewing the green paper.

Step four: I must make sure Pops is paying attention, so here's one last touch. These metal bows on his glasses. They don't taste good either, but this must be done.

Maybe while Pops is picking up this mess he'll listen to me.

MOM IS MISSING!
MOM IS MISSING!!
MOM! IS!! MISSING!!!

Guess what? I finally get Pop's attention and Mom is found. Pops gets up, looks at the mess and then looks at me. Why me? That goody two shoes Suni lives in this house too.

Quicker than a colt out of the chute, Pops picks up the phone. I hear Mom's voice on the other end, and my heart pounds with joy.

Pops says (with undue emphasis, I must say), "You have an expensive dog!" Then Pops explains why I am supposedly so expensive. I hear Mom laughing out loud. "Yeah, she's alive!" I tell my anxiety-ridden self. All I need to do now is figure out how to get her home from wherever she is. Because I got Pop's attention, Mom is found.

The Sequel:

It's been a week, but I feel less anxious. I know Mom is out there somewhere, because I hear her voice on the telephone.

I can't and won't believe she has left us, because she calls several times a day. Part of Mom's conversations are, "Hugs to the Bills and Sun Dog for me." I hear snatches of "Getting stronger . . . therapy . . . walked a thousand feet today." Whose feet? If they were mine (my paws), that wouldn't be very far.

I'm getting impatient. It's Thursday, and Mom's been gone a week. I'll give her until Sunday, and then I'll *really* get Pops attention.

Where's Mom?

Billie, the innocent, taking the blame

It's Not My Fault
By Billie

I am more adventuresome than my stodgy, boring "brother," so I get blamed for everything.

What is life if you don't take a chance? I've taken a few chances since I came to live with Pops and Mom. There was the billfold incident, the bows on the glasses, and chewing up the money, but I can assure you, I'm not always guilty.

Pops has a job that will be ending soon, so he has been filling out applications to various places for a new job. Well, the other night he left a fat old envelope with an application on the end table right beside the recliner. Now *I* wouldn't mess with that because if Pops doesn't have a job, we won't get dog food, especially the real quality stuff. Unfortunately, Suni lacks my superior wisdom.

The next morning when Mom got up to pack lunch and get breakfast for Pops, there it was. One application envelope totally chewed up and the application looking like someone tried and failed on shredding it with a paper shredder.

Of course, you know who got the blame – me, Wyldmore's Feature Storee, Billie, The Bills – all one and the same. Suddenly I became Pop's dog. I DIDN'T DO IT! But being the nearly perfect Puli I just lowered my head and walked into my crate and lay down.

And where is Suni when all this is going on? He's up in the bedroom innocently pretending to be fast asleep.

Mom starts in, "Jesse, your dog just chewed up your application." You the reader can fill in the rest because on and on she went.

Pops is a totally matter of fact sort of guy, so he tells Mom just to call for another one. Guess that's the old "the dog ate my homework" story. Then Pops gets up and takes the Sun Dog and me for a walk. Boy, did I give Suni an earful when we got outside! It was his first offense, and he could have looked a little guilty and not so goldurned proud that he'd gotten away with it.

You know the saying, "He who laughs last, laughs best?" Well, the next morning it was my turn to laugh. The night after "the incident" Mom had trouble sleeping. As luck would have it, she went down to the living room and nestled into the recliner.

Suni was asleep in Pops' recliner. I chased him out of his bed, and I wasn't even going to the living room that night. Mom was not quite asleep when I heard the Sun Dog get up and start nosing the paper on the end table. The paper wasn't important, but that wasn't the point. Then YEAH, I heard Mom say, "No!" Ha! Goody two shoes Suni was busted.

When morning came, Mom told Pops the truth and apologized to me. But I wonder why when I do something wrong Mom goes on and on, and when it is not my fault, all I get is just a single , "Good dog."

P.S. Suni didn't even get punished. He just got laughed at.

It's Not My Fault

Suni is saved from the leash.

Suni's Rescue
By Moms

This story is a copy of a letter written by the Mom of the flock, since Billie and Suni were both involved and you wouldn't get the same story from both of them. This way we know the story is accurate.

Dear Patty,

The Bills wanted me to pass along her Hi! She also needs to tell you she got in trouble the other day, although according to Pops, it was not Billie's fault. Pops had walked the dogs. They had messed, so when Pops brought them back, he just turned them loose in the house and went out to scoop poop.

Billie came to get her leash off and Suni went up to lie in his favorite spot – bed. I was busy and not paying close attention, since I was only a couple of minutes from finishing what I was doing.

Well, a couple of minutes was too long. Billie hopped off the bed and came to me dragging about two feet of leash. Oops.

Pops came in, and I showed him the piece of leash. He laughed and said not to be mad at Billie. Billie obviously thought Suni was caught, and it was her job to rescue him. Can you beat that?

The only good thing is we are in a little town called Van Horn, Texas, population 2,064. There's not much in this West Texas inferno other than distant views of Threemile Mountain and a lot of empty space. Van Horn is the last stop before nowhere. However, it has the one thing we needed: a saddle shop! And what do you find in a saddle shop? A lovely new genuine leather leash.

Suni's Rescue

I believe I told you about Billie tearing up Jesse's billfold and money when I was in the hospital. Pops took the money and put it in the safe in an envelope labeled, "Billie's savings."

I told Pops Billie could take responsibility and pay for her own mistakes, but Pops refused to open the safe. Instead, he paid for it. Billie "needs a nest egg." Oh, brother!!!

Rita (Mom of the flock)

"You know you want to take me home!"

Sucking in the Old Folks,
or Getting Adopted Made Easy

By Missy

"Hi there!" Welcome to my world. I do mean *world*, because I was born in Denmark and then came to the U.S. of A. Doesn't that make me a world traveler?

I am the sixth Puli to be a member of the Sikes' household. Please notice; "I did not say *owned* by the Sikes family. Nobody owns a Puli." Now that we have that straightened out and you understand how things are with Pulik, I will get on with my story.

I was living in a "dog house" when I met the Sikes folks. If I were to guess, I would say the dog house was approximately 1,400 sq. feet. Oh, did I say I shared this place with eight other Pulik, three Irish Wolfhounds, and two humans? I suppose some would consider that a human home full of dogs, but that is not the way it works in my world, the world of Missy the nearly perfect Puli. It was a Pulik home full of canine and human guests.

I was sunning myself, looking out the sliding glass doors at the Rocky Mountains, when the phone rang. I didn't bother getting up. It was Miz Barb's job to answer the phone.

I truly wasn't interested in the conversation, but I did catch snatches. Miz Barb said something to the effect of, "Oh, do come visit. Suni is more than welcome. I haven't seen you two in several years." I thought to myself, "These folks may be welcome, but leave that dog at home!"

A few weeks go by, and here comes an older gentleman and a short chunky lady with much too loud a laugh. Trotting beside them, looking rather superior was butter-wouldn't-melt-in-his-mouth Suni Puli. Well *I'll* soon wipe that smirk off his face. (Yes, dogs can smirk. If you don't believe that, then you don't know much about the dog world and the sophistication of canine non-verbal communication.)

Sucking in the Old Folks

Little did these folks know the plan was already in place. Right after that fatal phone call, the wheels went into motion. Miz Barb had told me the story behind these old geezers. She said they needed me and proceeded to explain why.

Over the course of twenty-seven years Pulik have been a part of the Sikes' household. LuBove (Luba Lu), the first one, arrived to cheer Kelly the five-year old girl kid whose Dad had passed away.

Four years passed, and the Boss Lady remarried the man who became known as Pops to us. Pops had a son Sam, and of course Miz Barb thought Sam needed a Puli. Miz Barb lived in California and told Pops and the Boss Lady (later known as Mom) that she would fly two Pulik to Wyoming and they could take their pick and send one back.

Right. That never happened. Fred and Smokey became part of the family. After the Rainbow Bridge called Luba, Fred, and Smokey home, Billy and Suni arrived. Billy departed to the Rainbow Bridge and Miz Barb thought Pops and Suni needed a friend.

Miz Barb chose me because I had paid my dues. As I said, I was born in Denmark, spent time as a show dog, and raised a couple litters of pups. It was time to find my forever home. After all I am a bit long in the tooth. (9), so I knew I had to make a plan.

I obediently waited in the "dog room." I let Miz Barb greet her friends and get them coffee. My observations tell me coffee fixes anything. I heard Miz Barb tell about me in glowing terms. What other terms are there for a nearly perfect Puli? Next Miz Barb opened the door and nine of us rushed into the room.

I want you to know this plan had been in the works for a couple of weeks, ever since I overheard the phone call. I'd had a serious talk in the dog yard with the others, and they knew what to do. Serious talk; "Grr, grr, snap, snap, woof, "back-off he's-mine-type talk.

Everyone trotted into the room and gave Pops and Mom a sniff and went and lay down. That is, everyone except me. I sniffed Mom first and then honed in on my prey, Pops. Sniff, nudge, get a pat, nudge again and plop at his feet. I see a smile and know this sucker is mine.

Sucking in the Old Folks

Remember that "fatal" phone call? Fatal for Pops, that is. He's been had. Someone once said "A sucker is born every minute." Pops just goes to prove that theory.

I'll tolerate Suni and Mom, of course. But Pops is *mine*. My new home is The Cowboy State. We'll see what adventures await in Wyoming.

"Training the people you own makes
for harmony in the household."

Training People
By Missy

Training your people can be difficult and time-consuming. It's a job that requires the patience of a Puli. The Pulik are a very patient folk as you know, because how else could you deal with a large flock of sheep falling all over their own wooly hooves?

The first principle is to train your folks one at a time. People are actually more difficult than sheep. Do not attempt obedience training with more than one at a time.

The second principle is to take the time to closely observe the behavior of your human group. It is critical to identify the one who will cave most quickly. Once the decision is made you can set about your task with zeal and complete confidence.

As you may know from my reputation, I am Millie/Missy, the nearly perfect Puli dog. It is my understanding that Pulik can do anything. Here's how I set about my training responsibilities with the Sikes family.

The primary task: Teach my folks that my being on the sofa is not a bad thing. It is where all dogs should be, regardless of size or length of hair.

My method of sofa training, stage one: I started out by being good and lying on the floor. I pretended this was the best place to be. The very middle of the floor is a perfect choice; my people noticed me since they had to walk around or step over my furry body. Stretching and yawning once in a while worked to ensure that my presence was more frequently acknowledged.

Stage two: After a few days of being casual I, the nearly perfect Puli, moved in for the kill. Pops made the mistake of sitting on the sofa instead of sitting in his recliner. What an opportunity!

Training People

I was in the middle of the floor stretching and yawning to get attention. Pops noticed and said, "Missy, come here." Being the obedient dog that I am, I immediately responded.

Oops! I swear it was an accident, but my paws, followed by my body in one elegantly fluid movement, landed on the sofa beside Pops. Without thinking he reached over to pat me. Enough said. It only took this one training session to let him know the sofa was "My Place." After all, no one needs to walk around me on the floor any more. What a convenience. Hah!

Enough for now – later – Woof! May paw prints always walk through your heart.

Miss Millie, Missy,
aka Bubbleton's
Millenium Celebration

"I can't believe I ate the whole thing."

The Benefits of Careful Observation

By Suni

Missy thinks I am just a casual observer of life, since my main perches are the bed or the recliner. I can attest, however, that there are many lessons to be learned by being a casual observer.

The following event is an example of learning by example of what not to do. I'm here to tell you all the facts are absolutely true.

We were in Benson, Arizona for the winter. It was a bit cool outdoors, almost on the cold side, the kind of weather when something baking in the oven gives you a case of the warm fuzzies. The Mom of the flock decided to be domesticated and bake bread. Well, that is to almost bake bread.

Seven Nearly Perfect Pulik

Let's face it. Mom went to the freezer department of the grocery store and bought one of those frozen loaves you thaw, let rise and bake.

Adept in the kitchen Mom is not. First she took the loaf of frozen bread put it in the bread pan and thawed the bread. Next, Mom turned the pilot light on in the oven. Now for me this is a no brainer. You let the bread rise in the warm oven. With only the pilot light on, it should not bake. But what do I know? I am only Suni the nearly perfect Puli.

Time went by, and the bread was not rising as quickly as the Mom of the flock thought it should, patience in the kitchen not being her long suit.

To this day I do not know what possessed Mom, but in her infinite wisdom she decided to put the bread on the floor on the register since the furnace was on. Well, the bread continued to rise and was about half its finished size.

As all of you have gathered from my previous writings, I am an observer of life, but Missy is a take-charge-get-to-it dog.

The real-time scenario: Pops is asleep in the recliner in front of the TV. Mom is working on the computer while supposedly watching the bread, so we dogs would stay out of it.

Well, sometimes Mom gets way too involved. She does not see Missy creep up and gobble down three-quarters of the rising loaf of bread. All of a sudden Mom looks up and gasps. Pops springs awake. Missy is looking very uncomfortable and she now resembles a barrel. If I had pushed her with my nose she would have rolled across the floor.

Mom springs into action. Aren't Mom's always supposed to spring into action when there is a crisis? She tells Pops, "Get her outside on a leash! I will be right there." Mom heads for the medicine cabinet and comes back with hydrogen peroxide and a syringe. "What end does that go in?" I wonder. Oh Missy! This time I really feel sorry for you. Mom heads outside and I am guessing it was the front end because very shortly I hear Missy upchucking and upchucking.

Mom runs in, heads for the phone, and calls the vet. Mom tells them all the vital information and the next thing I know we are in the pick-up headed for Tucson at a very unrealistic rate of speed. Where is a cop when you need one? Probably just as well. Mr. Highway Patrolman might not have considered a sick dog a reason for speeding or a reason to give an escort.

Pops pulls into the vet's. I find myself locked in the pick-up as Mom, Pops and Missy waddle into the vets. (Actually Missy and Mom were the only ones waddling.)

With my keen ears and the window cracked I hear the best part of the conversation. The vet tech looks up from her desk and says, "Hi! You must be the Sikes, and this must be the Pillsbury Dough Dog."

P.S. The vet kept Missy overnight and she was fine the next day. Looked a little sheepish, but fine. I have come to the conclusion that she is a little dense. When we got home, she made a dive for the pile of regurgitated dough that ended up outside the trailer. Looking up at me with a sickly and slightly apologetic smile, she muttered, "It's addictive. Not my fault."

The Benefits of Careful Observation

Obedience Personified (Most of the time!)

Obedience, Obedience
By Bari

As much as I love Mom and Pops, I must say Mom is like a Pit Bull with a bone. When she gets something in her head, she just doesn't let it go. In a Pit Bull I would call that intelligent determination. In Mom I would call it bullheaded stubbornness. Most of the time Pops will just smile and go along with Mom's ideas.

First let me state my disclaimer on this missive. I did not need to be the target of this project of Mom's, nor did I ask for it.

I came to Mom and Pops at five months old. Miz Barb told me this was the perfect home. Over the last five years I found that to be the case. Pats and belly rubs are abundant. When I went home with Mom and Pops I already knew how to "sit," "down," "come," and "stay" (sometimes).

But Mom has this preconceived idea of how I should behave in public. No jumping, no spinning, no barking and no crocodile snapping. What fun is that? Crocodile snapping is when my jaws snap three times. I never grab anything; I just snap. And I never, but never, snap more than three times. I do it when I'm nervous, happy, or just want to play.

When I'm out with Pops walking I get really excited when I see other dogs. So I jump and bark saying, "Come see me, let's be friends." However, most of the dogs are little, and the owners and their dogs turn and go the other way. So Mom decides I need help.

We are in Evanston, Wyoming, and here comes dog obedience 101. Private lessons in our back yard. Well, heck! In your own back yard for treats and a little click sound? "Why not? I can do this," I say to myself. And I aced that one.

After winter in Arizona, a job calls Pops name in Sacramento, CA. We head for a great RV park there. Lots of people. There is much to bark at and lunge at.

Obedience, Obedience

Oops! Training. Is training transferable from Wyoming to California? Mom is at it again. A lady comes to the house. This is a piece of cake. Just like last time, "Sit, down, stay, come, and heel." Aced it again, except maybe the "heel." That means I'm to walk beside Mom and not get too far forward. But the world awaits out there and Mom walks slow. For the final test, I behaved.

Time passes. My brain says behave, and my feet and mouth don't listen. Off we go again. This time there are no treats and a pinch collar is involved. I walk into a class of Rotweilers, Pit Bulls and German Shepherds. I, the nearly perfect Puli, am the smallest dog there. Misbehave? Why on earth would I misbehave? I'm with the big boys.

Can you believe it? I happen to be the best dog in the class. Even my heel is good here. Those big boys walk within a foot of my nose. Somehow my crocodile snap just won't work. Mom never did get to use the pinch collar. It turned out to be just a handsome piece of macho canine jewelry.

More time passes. It is winter in southern Arizona. Spring arrives and Pops is off on another job.

You ask, "Why do you live in an RV?" Well, it's hard to tow a house if it doesn't have wheels. This time it's Casper, Wyoming. Mom is bored. She has read and computed all she can. That means I become the next project.

Why me? There are no dogs in this park for me to scare, and all the men go to work everyday. I am being a good dog. Again, why me?

Naturally, all works out fine. I put my best paw forward and ace this one more time. How many times do we have to do this? I guess if it keeps Mom happy, then Pops is happy, and life is good.

Now we are in Tucson, Arizona. Pops is working on another pipeline job. We are living in an RV park out in the middle of the desert. Cactus, birds, bunnies, and lizards abound. There's even an occasional snake. Mom decides on private lessons. This is treat and clicker based.

You know, maybe these obedience lessons are not a bad thing. All those treats on top of my regular meals. Look interested, get food. What is wrong with that?

Obedience, Obedience

There is an added wrinkle to these particular lessons. The German Shepherd dogs that are used to distract me are training for Schutzhund work. These dogs are really bouncy. I must admit I forgot to stay down the first time one of these guys bounced by. But then I decided that observation of this behavior was fun, so I just lay there and let them act goofy. I was told Schutzhund training has a purpose, but it looks like bouncy fun to me. It also looks like a lot of work.

I am just starting another obedience class. Mom must be really bored this year. Two classes in one summer. This is a group class. I am the biggest dog there. I've only been to the first class. Basically it is the same stuff, different day. But if it gets Mom out and keeps her happy, why not?

I will just go back to doing what I want to do when it is over. I'll consider myself a work in progress.

Pops said he is considering changing my name to "Money Pit." Well again, I want you to know it's not my fault. Mom is the one with the problem.

Seven Nearly Perfect Pulik

CPSIA information can be obtained at www.ICGtesting.com
Printed in the USA
BVOW11*1203201114

375602BV00001BA/1/P

9 781634 431613